YELLOW
OVERALLS

The King of Biddlikurri
and the King of Gunjee
had an argument.

"I declare war on you!"
shouted the King of Biddlikurri.

"And I declare war on you!"
yelled the King of Gunjee.
"When do we go to battle?"

"On Saturday morning!"
shouted the King of Biddlikurri.

In the town of Biddlikurri,
five hundred soldiers got ready for war.
They polished boots and guns.
Then they paraded through the town
in their new red uniforms.

"We will win!" cried the King of Biddlikurri.

In Gunjee, five hundred soldiers
got dressed in their new blue uniforms.

They beat their drums and marched
up and down, clicking their heels.

"Victory is ours!" cried the King of Gunjee.

Now, this was bad news
for the Queen of Gunjee
and the Queen of Biddlikurri,
who were very good friends.

"When there's a war on,
we can't talk to each other,"
sighed the Queen of Biddlikurri.

"War is stupid," said the Queen
of Gunjee. "It shouldn't be allowed."

"It puts my husband in a bad mood,"
said the Queen of Biddlikurri.

"It ruins my husband's uniform,"
the Queen of Gunjee said.

The Queen of Biddlikurri smiled.
"Uniforms!" she said. "That's it!"

"That's what?" asked her friend.

"Uniforms! Uniforms!"
The Queen of Biddlikurri walked
around and around, laughing to herself.
"We'll need lots of cloth.
The soldiers' wives will help us."

"Help us to do what?"
said the Queen of Gunjee.

The Queen of Biddlikurri bent over
and whispered the plan
in her friend's ear.

That same day, the two friends
went shopping in a distant city.
They came back with
a truckload of yellow cloth.

The next morning, each queen
took the cloth to the soldiers'
wives in her own town.

All over Gunjee and
Biddlikurri, the wives secretly
snipped and sewed, snipped
and sewed, while their
husbands prepared for battle.

The night before the battle, the Queen of Biddlikurri crept out of the castle. She went to the rooms where the soldiers' red uniforms were hung up in rows.

She took out the sharp scissors she had hidden in her hair.

Meanwhile, the Queen of
Gunjee sneaked out of her
castle. She went past the
guards and into the rooms
where the soldiers'
blue uniforms hung
ready for war.

The Queen of Gunjee
took a sharp knife
from her royal belt.

The following day,
the soldiers dressed for battle.

In the town of Biddlikurri,
there rose a loud cry.
"Our uniforms! Look! The rats have been
eating our beautiful, new red uniforms!
We can't go to war like this!"

"Don't worry," said the queen.
"I've got some nice yellow overalls.
There'll be enough for all of you."

"Yellow overalls!" moaned the king.

"Yellow overalls!" groaned the soldiers.

"Better than going to war in your
underwear," said the Queen of Biddlikurri.

In the town of Gunjee, the soldiers
ran to their king. "Just look at us!
The moths have had a feast of our brand-
new blue uniforms. They're in rags!"

"Mine, too!" said the king.
"What can we wear to battle?"

"Here is the answer—" said the queen,
"smart yellow overalls to fit all of you."

"Yellow overalls!" grumbled the king.

"Yellow overalls!" mumbled the soldiers.

"Better than going to war
in your birthday suits," said the queen.

The King of Biddlikurri and his men
marched out of the town and down
to the battlefield.

The King of Gunjee and his men
marched out to meet them.

Two streams of yellow overalls flowed
down the hillsides and met at the bottom.

But which side was which?
No one could tell.
They were all dressed alike.

The King of Biddlikurri shouted
to the King of Gunjee, "How can we
fight when we all look as though
we're on the same side?"

"Where did you get your overalls?"
said the King of Gunjee.

"From my wife,"
replied the King of Biddlikurri.
"Where did you get yours?"

"One guess!" said the King of Gunjee.

"Oh-oh!" they both said.

The soldiers soon got tired
of trying to fight when they
didn't know who they were fighting.

In the end, they all sat
on the ground, looking like
buttercups, and had a picnic.

The Queen of Biddlikurri
and the Queen of Gunjee
watched them.

"Yellow is so beautiful," they said.

STEPS TO READING

GW00801690

Dear Parent:

Congratulations! Your child is taking the first steps on an exciting journey **The destination? Independent reading!**

STEPS TO READING will help your child get there. The programme offers three steps to reading success. Each step includes fun stories and colourful art, and the result is a complete literacy programme with something for every child.

Learning to Read, Step by Step!

① **Start to Read   Nursery – Preschool**
• **big type and easy words** • **rhyme and rhythm** • **picture clues**
For children who know the alphabet and are eager to begin reading.

② **Let's read together   Preschool – Year 1**
• **basic vocabulary** • **short sentences** • **simple stories**
For children who recognise familiar words and sound out new words with help.

③ **I can read by myself   Years 1-3**
• **engaging characters** • **easy-to-follow plots** • **popular topics**
For children who are ready to read on their own.

STEPS TO READING is designed to give every child a successful reading experience. The year levels are only guides. Children can progress through the steps at their own speed, developing confidence in their reading, no matter what their year.

***Remember, a lifetime love of reading
starts with a single step!***

By Andrea Posner-Sanchez
Illustrated by Isidre Monés

This edition published by Parragon in 2011

Parragon
Queen Street House
4 Queen Street
Bath BA1 1HE, UK

ISBN 978-1-4454-2108-7

Printed in Malaysia

Bambi's Hide
and Seek

Bath · New York · Singapore · Hong Kong · Cologne · Delhi
Melbourne · Amsterdam · Johannesburg · Auckland · Shenzhen

Bambi.

Thumper.

Hide-and-seek!

Counting.

Hiding.

Is that Thumper
behind the bush?

That is not Thumper!

"Shh!"

14

Inside the tree?

Nuts!

16

That is not Thumper!

In the creek?

That is not Thumper!

"Ribbit!"

By the log?

Tap, tap, tap.

"You are not Thumper!" says Bambi.

Bambi rests.

"Achoo!"

29

There is Thumper!

"Let's play again!"

Now turn
over for the
next story...

By Jennifer Liberts Weinberg
Illustrated by Carlo LoRaso and John Kurtz

Ⓓⁱˢⁿᵉʸ

DUMBO

Fly Dumbo, Fly

PaRRagon

Bath · New York · Singapore · Hong Kong · Cologne · Delhi
Melbourne · Amsterdam · Johannesburg · Auckland · Shenzhen

Who are you?

Dumbo!

"Achoo!"

Oh, dear.
Big ears.

41

A parade!

Oh, dear.

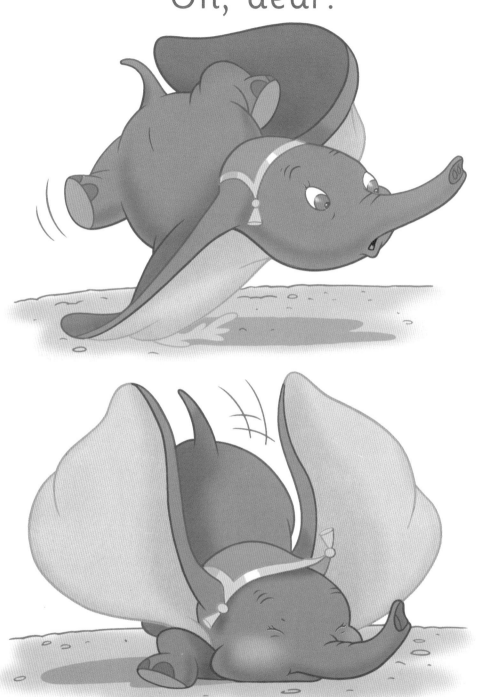

Those ears!

Poor Dumbo.

Who is there?

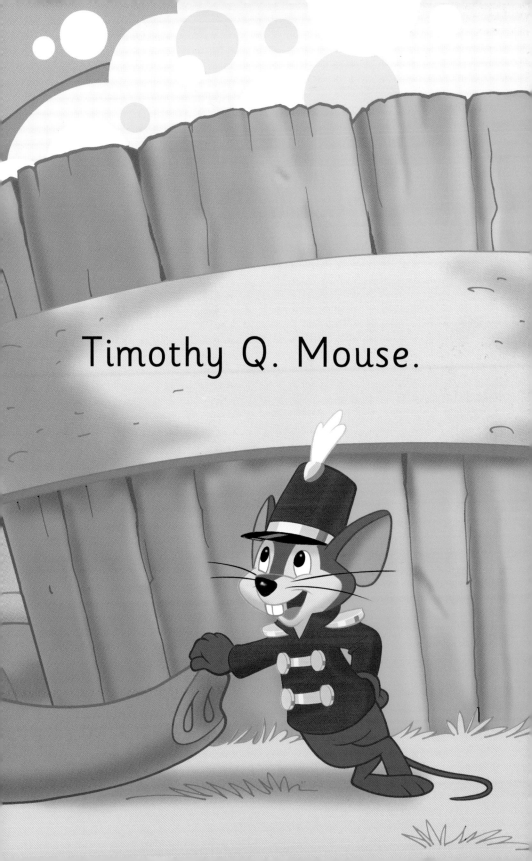

Timothy Q. Mouse.

"Cheer up, Dumbo!"

Friends!

Dumbo tries.

Dumbo trips!

Aha!

Wings!

"Jump, Dumbo!"

Down, down, down.

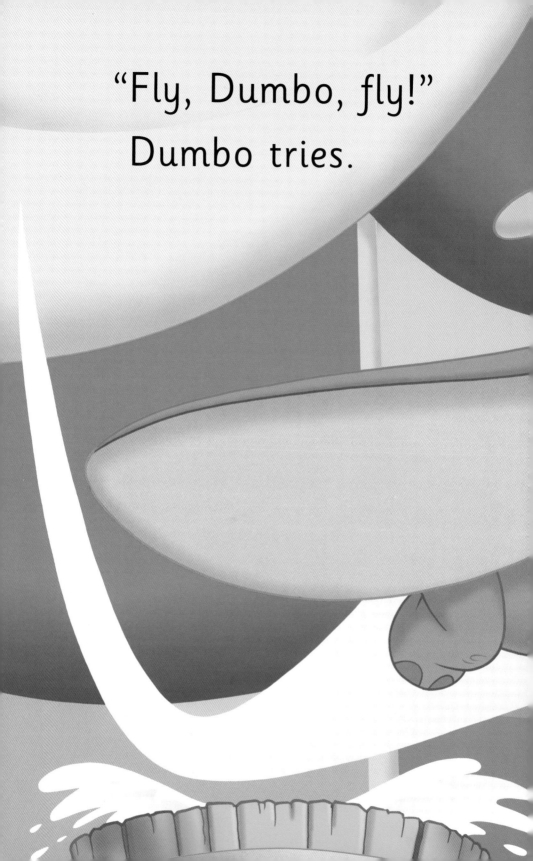

"Fly, Dumbo, fly!"
Dumbo tries.

Up, up, up.
Dumbo flies!

Loop-the-loop!

"Well done, Dumbo!"